WILD WATER · WILD LIGHT

IMAGES OF THE WEST CORK COASTLINE

Mike Brown

WILD WATER · WILD LIGHT

IMAGES OF THE WEST CORK COASTLINE

Mike Brown

MIKE BROWN

PHOTOGRAPHY

Published in 2009 by Mike Brown Photography
Ashe St, Clonakilty, Co. Cork, Ireland

Design by Ramona Stafford Ryan
@ Mike Brown Photography

Pre press consultant Patryk Lubas

All photographs copyright Mike Brown

Catalogue in publication. A CIP catalogue record for this book is
available from the British Library.

ISBN 0-978-0-9542863-2-3

Prints from this book may be purchased by contacting
Mike Brown Photography on +353 88 23 35782 or at
www.mikebrownphotography.com

Contents

FOR MY MUM ANNABEL
AND MY LATE GRANDPARENTS DENNIS AND PATRICIA,
FOR BRINGING ME TO THIS WONDERFUL PLACE

SPONSOR & COMMERCIAL PATRONS

This book would not have been possible without the generous assistance of my main sponsor and the Commercial Patrons listed below. I wish to express my eternal thanks to them all for their support.

I would like to say a special thanks to Bob and Maria for their support on this project.

Courtmacsherry
• Hotel •
& Coastal Cottages

courtmacsherryhotel@eircom.net
tel: 023 88 46198

82 North Main St.
Bandon, Co.Cork

Quality Value Service

Mullins | Lynch | Byrne
(Incorporating Dillon Mullins)
SOLICITORS

Melbourne House, Model Farm Road, Cork.

Website: www.mlbsolicitors.ie Email: firstnamesurname@mlbsolicitors.ie

Tel: 021 434 0315 Fax: 021 434 6100

INTRODUCTION

The Book

West Cork is huge. Its coastline seems to go on forever. Meandering in and out constantly, it is an almost infinite collection of tiny bays, inlets and harbours, punctuated by headlands, points and promontories. Some of these are easily accessible, while others are hidden away down lanes and boreens that only the hardened traveller will follow. Arriving at the end of one of these tiny roads, a walk is often needed to find the best viewpoint. Indeed some of the most picturesque and interesting places on this coastline are best viewed from the sea. Add to that the multitude of islands that are dotted along its length and it becomes obvious

that no book could cover all of this sufficiently and in a way that truly does it justice. There are small coves and beaches I know of, that would supply me with enough photographic opportunities to keep me going for a lifetime and could certainly warrant a book to themselves. Then of course there are the villages. Brightly coloured pubs and houses, quirky signs and interesting shop windows. These are the trademarks of West Cork and this is often the way it

is portrayed. For a project like this it would be tempting to photograph many of these usual viewpoints and scenes. If I were to choose sunny summer days with blue skies, dotted with puffy white clouds, it would be easy to see what a wonderful place we live in. However, I am motivated more by the wild beauty of this coastline and prefer to look at it from a slightly different viewpoint.

As a nature photographer I have travelled this county and indeed this country quite extensively. What always strikes me about West Cork and particularly its coast is the sense of wilderness. Pure, wild and weather beaten with a feeling of quiet emptiness. This is what I have attempted to photograph in this book. To keep within the confines of a book of this size some decisions had to be made. I chose to stick with just the mainland coastline in this book rather than including the islands. This may disappoint some people but my feeling was that they are so numerous they surely deserve a book of their own and I will hopefully attempt this in the future. Apart from some

slightly artistic interpretations and some very distant views, I also chose to omit the villages and towns along the way. They have all been photographed extensively in the past for books and other projects and I didn't want to repeat the work of others. So I would stick to wild places along our coast. Some of the views I have chosen are well known but I have tried to show them in a new way. Others are only seen by those who choose to search them out. I will of course have missed out on some favoured spots but hopefully this book will give you some new and undiscovered viewpoints. Lastly, the little details I have chosen to include. I adore beach combing and rock hopping along our coast, searching out things to photograph along the way. Scraps of rope or discarded fishing equipment that washes up on the shoreline. Fishing nets lying tangled and idle. Dead bodies and skeletons of boats that once served well for work or pleasure. Seaweed clinging to a rock or kelp discarded by the dropping tide. Tiny details on the rocky shorelines or just wild wintery days on beaches that we mostly enjoy on the balmy days of summer. These are all beautiful to my eye and I consider them to be one of the bonuses of living in this special place.

cannot pass a body of water of any size, shape or form without wondering if its worth having a cast or two. Living on the coast that temptation is always there but these days I enjoy the sea for many other reasons too. It is a constant inspiration for my photography and of course it is home to many of the creatures that I photograph in my wildlife work. Its mood can change from pleasant to savage in a matter of hours as a weather front moves in and the wind gets up. It can soothe the senses by just observing its constant movement but it can be a frightening force of nature which cares not for those who don't respect it. It is this wild beauty that I yearn to capture in my images.

How I came to be here.

For most of my life I have been a fisherman. I received my first fishing rod for my fourth birthday. My father had been fishing for many years and I was now able to accompany him on trips to the local lakes and gravel pits in Yorkshire where I was born. I would fish for small perch while he searched for more serious creatures of the deep. I mention this because it is very relevant to the relationship I have with the sea. As anybody who has ever had the fishing "bug" knows, a fisherman

I was thirteen years old when my grandparents Dennis and Patricia Adams instigated a family move to Courtmacsherry. They had been coming to Ireland since 1960 and had discovered "Courtmac" at the start of the 70's. They had decided to purchase the small hotel there for my uncle Terry to run. They would essentially be retired but would help with the day to day running of the hotel and meet and greet the guests. My father had died a few years earlier and my mother, my sister and I decided to make the move too. I was attending a boarding school in the city of York, and the family moved over during my spring term in 1974. When the Easter holiday arrived, I travelled alone to Ireland, something which railway station was followed by what I thought at the time was a never ending train journey to Cork. I was met by my mother who drove me on the final leg of the journey to our new home in the village of Courtmacsherry. As an energetic teenager, I was still

would probably not be done these days. I took a train to Liverpool where I boarded the ferry for Dublin. After arrival at the Dublin docks, a bus to Heuston alert even after such a long and tiring journey and I was full of excitement at the prospect of seeing the small seaside village I had heard so much about. As we arrived in Timoleague I caught my first glimpse of the water. Heading down the narrow, winding coastal road to Courtmacsherry the realisation that I was about to start living in such close proximity to the sea began to sink in. Thoughts of what wonderful fish might exist in this place filled my mind. In the thirty five years that have passed since I first set eyes on Courtmacsherry and the West Cork coast, I have indeed done quite a lot of fishing. This has been very enjoyable but it is now far outweighed by the simple sense of wonder I feel at living in such an incredible place.

During this time here our family has increased and more of us have invaded this part of the world. Terry, my uncle who has run the hotel in Courtmacsherry since our arrival, married Carole and their children were born and raised here. Their daughter Siobhan now has her own daughter Izzie. Their son Billy now runs the hotel. My sister Kate has married Padjoe a born and reared West Cork man and is raising her family close by in Clonakilty. My mother's sister and her husband moved here soon after the rest of us and after taking a few years away for work purposes have returned to settle. Their three children, the last of whom was born here, are also all living in Ireland and two have families of their own. So there's quite a clan here after 35 years or so. The reason for writing about this is that we are not unique in this respect. From Kinsale to Eyeries in the far west, I meet people of all nationalities who have chosen to live in this wonderful place. It has become truly cosmopolitan and this is a testament to the friendly and accepting nature of the people of West Cork. But without doubt the wonderful spirit of this coastal landscape is also what draws people here. I hope it is always so.

Making the Photographs

Landscape photography is best carried out at the cusp of the day. The Earth looks better in the early morning and late evening and these are usually the most dramatic times of day. In West Cork it is no different. Yellow-orange dawns that promise so much but often deliver a less than perfect day. Skies that turn to blood red as the sun shows itself briefly just before sinking beyond the horizon. Our weather can change from heavy rain to bright sunshine in a blink and sometimes it is not possible to predict

how or when. Areas like the Beara peninsula have their own micro climates due to their mountainous topography and their coastal placement. It can be pouring on one side of Bantry Bay and glorious sunshine on the other. This is what I wanted to record in this book. This wonderful mix of light and water. It can be frustrating. Being on the edge of the Atlantic Ocean and influenced by the warm Gulf Stream we can have long periods of mild, grey, moist weather. Even periods of consistent high pressure can be useless for photography. The haze

associated with these warm, dry periods makes it impossible to record detail in distant backgrounds. Many days that I travelled west from my home near Timoleague were wasted due to these difficult and unsuitable weather conditions. Watching weather forecasts can help but I have often been scuppered by the timing of a change in the conditions. But this location of ours gives us some incredible spectacles too. Skies that are indescribably beautiful can form as the pressure changes and good weather turns bad. Being there at these moments is one of my greatest pleasures and recording it for others to experience is my aim. And then there is the sea. Its influence on my work is profound. Each time I drive a coastal road I will be checking its mood. Whether wild and aggressive or calm and benign it is always interesting. This is my West Cork, I hope you like it.

"At times, it is enough just to be there. On other occasions I feel it would be a crime not to attempt to capture the wild beauty of this special place."

I am never quite sure where West Cork actually starts. For his book I decided that the western side of the Old Head of Kinsale would be a good place. On this spring evening I was hoping for some interesting clouds but the sky stayed clear. As evening fell the setting sun sent a pink glow across the hazy sky and the waves blended together as I used a slow shutter speed on the camera to record their movement.

16

The old breakwater catches the light on Garrettstown beach on a beautiful calm evening.

A layer of seaweed clings to the rock.

Waves push high on the rocks on a stormy evening near the western end of Garrettstown beach

The old Coast Guard building at Howe strand catches the light at the end of a wild day in winter.

First light on a beautiful morning at Harbour view near Kilbrittain.

Timoleague abbey reflects in the estuary on a perfect still night.

This dramatic sunset over Courtmacsherry harbour is one of the most vivid I have ever seen anywhere. The colour of the sky was simply incredible and no filter was used for this image.

This is the oldest shot in this book but I felt I had to include it. We seldom get real snow on the West Cork coastline due to the warming effect of the Gulf Stream, so to see it so close to the beach in Broadstrand on this occasion was a special treat.

Hard stones made smooth by the constant attention of the tide.

Looking in towards Blind strand just after first light on a glorious morning.

Dawn breaks at Travara on the Seven heads.

Pastel pinks and purples fill the sky over the old watch tower at Leganagh point on the Seven heads.

Rough seas pound the rocks at Dunworley point on spring afternoon.

A collection of multi coloured pebbled deposited by the sea.

A stunning sunset over Dunworley beach, a popular destination for both locals and visitors in this area of West Cork.

Late on a March afternoon the sun lights up the landscape at Lissycrimeen.

The last rays of sunshine catch the shoreline at Donaghmore near Ballinglanna.

A wild and stormy sea at Simon's Cove as a winter morning begins.

The other side of Simon's Cove on a calm and quiet evening.

Erupting like a spouting geyser, a wave is forced through a blow hole created over thousands of years by the relentless motion of the waves.
Pages 38 & 39 - Looking across Clonakilty Bay from the western side of Sheep Cove, known by many as Nun's Cove, as the sun goes down.

Stones and pebbles nestle into a wave shaped line of rock.

Sensational light at Ring pier
in Clonakilty Harbour warns
of a change in the weather.

Looking out onto the beach at Inchydoney from the Virgin Mary's Bank early on a beautiful November morning.

A glorious sunrise viewed from Muckruss Head by Dunmore.

A bright red periwinkle sticks to a heavily marked rock on the shoreline.

Looking East across Clonakilty Bay over a large bloom of wild poppies above the small beach at Duneen.

Late evening sunlight glances off the rocks at the eastern end of Red strand with the Galley Head lighthouse visible in the distance.

Hidden away at the western end of Red strand and not visible from the beach itself is this beautiful natural rock arch.
I chose to photograph this as night fell.

A wide view of the Galley Head lighthouse from the western side.

Beautiful clouds and soft light over Rosscarbery Bay.

After a long day of flat dull weather this strange and almost scary sky suddenly formed in the late afternoon of a December day. Using strong filters to lessen the contrast I was able to shoot against the light and still show the almost white rocks at the eastern end of the Long strand.

Simple and perfect.

A sublime sunset at Owenahincha. Three fellow photographers who were attending one of my workshops on this particular evening should have very similar images in their photo albums!

Just after sunrise on a bright and beautiful morning at the Warren in Rosscarbery, one of West Cork's most popular beaches.

Go down a tiny winding road near Glandore and you find Tralong Bay. Walk out along the shoreline from the small slipway and you will come across a group of extra large boulders covered in yellow lichens and a lovely view of the cliffs opposite.

Looking across the mouth of Glandore Harbour from the high cliffs at Goat's Head. These clouds will bring rain soon.

A sunrise like this one at Squince Harbour, Myross, makes getting up at 4.00am truly worthwhile.

The rising sun shines down the length of Castle Haven but bands of dark cloud at sea suggest the day may not stay so fine.

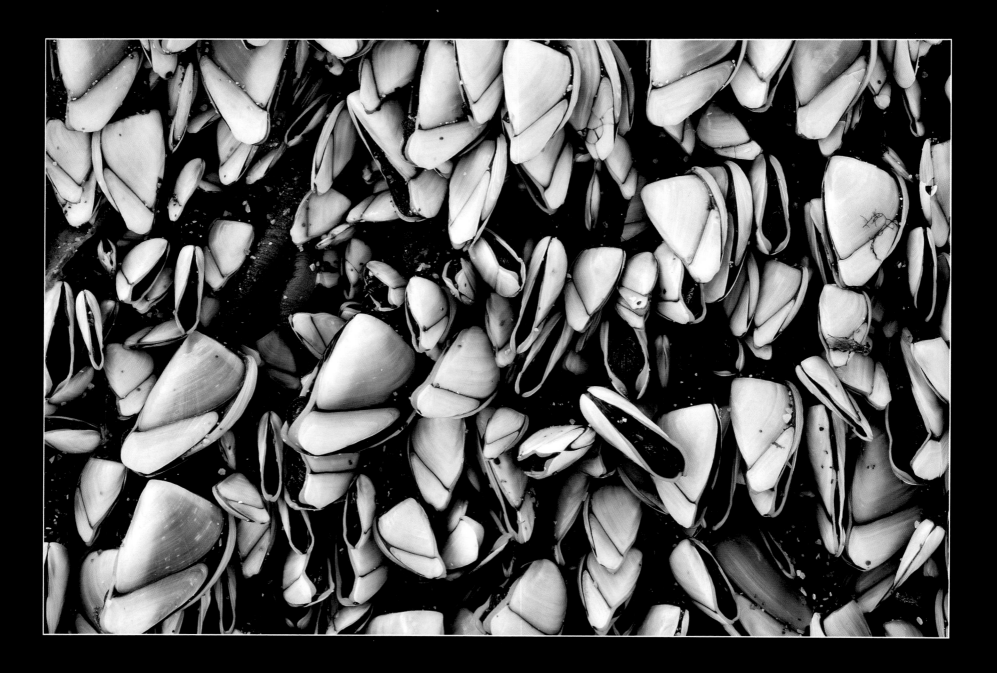

EVER THE NATURE PHOTOGRAPHER, I DECIDED TO INCLUDE A SMALL SELECTION
OF IMAGES OF THE WILD INHABITANTS OF OUR COASTLINE.

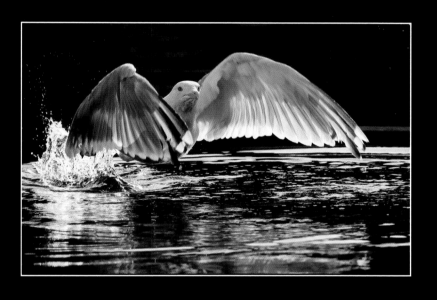

Looking across from Sandycove, the distinctive shape of Toe Head is silhouetted against a vibrant sky just after the sun has dropped out of sight.

An unusually calm sea greets me on a bright morning out at Toe Head.

Gentle waves push up the small beach facing out into Toe Head Bay on a perfect night.

Walking out along the rocks from the car park at Tragumna I had a feeling that my morning would be in vain. Shortly after first light the drizzle stopped and the clouds to the west caught a hint of colour. Everything came good after all.

A peaceful dawn at Lough Hyne.

A panoramic view of the Beacon at Baltimore and Sherkin Island as the winter sunlight disappears.

On the hill above the small pier at Turk Head, the view across Roaringwater Bay is dominated by huge rocks.

I returned to Turk Head on another evening in Autumn and photographed the view out towards Cape Clear as the sunlight raked across the landscape and coloured the gathering clouds.

There is beauty in everything if we take the time to look.

An almost vicious sunset over Heir Island.

Kilcoe castle dominates the landscape in the soft morning light.

The day begins at the twelve arch bridge at Ballydehob.

The day closed in and went grey as I arrived at Castle Point, West of Schull. The sea was so calm however, that I decided to make an almost abstract and monochrome image of the Promontory Fort on this narrow headland.

Soft light on the rocks in front of the wedge tomb at Altar on the Goleen road from Schull.

Shadows fall on the small beach at Toormore Bay at the end of a beautiful Autumn day.

A small stream makes beautiful patterns in the sand en route to the sea.

A beautiful orange dawn at the pier in Crookhaven.

The sea in motion on the road outside Crookhaven on a wild winter night.

Weeks of waiting for the best weather paid off, as a dawn visit to the Fastnet Rock produced this stunning image of the lighthouse. Colin Barnes who took me there told me that in nearly 20 years of being at sea he could hardly remember a morning so beautiful.

A fantastic storm builds at Barleycove.
Pages 90 & 91 - The power and the glory of the Ocean.

Made by the waves.

Lissagriffin on a beautiful morning.

The Mizen Head lighthouse as the first rays of light break through the cloud.

Large waves break over the rocks in Dunlough Bay on a wonderful West Cork evening.

This rock pavement has taken on the appearance of the waves that shaped it.

Rough seas swirl and boil on a blue evening at Toor Point on the North side of the Mizen peninsula.

Looking across Dunmanus Bay in Autumn.

A rainbow warns of an oncoming shower on the road between Durrus and Ahakista.

A stream runs over the rocks to the shoreline after heavy rain.

This old boat near Ahakista is often photographed but I wanted to include it as it I find the colours of the peeling paint and the rusted nails so beautiful.

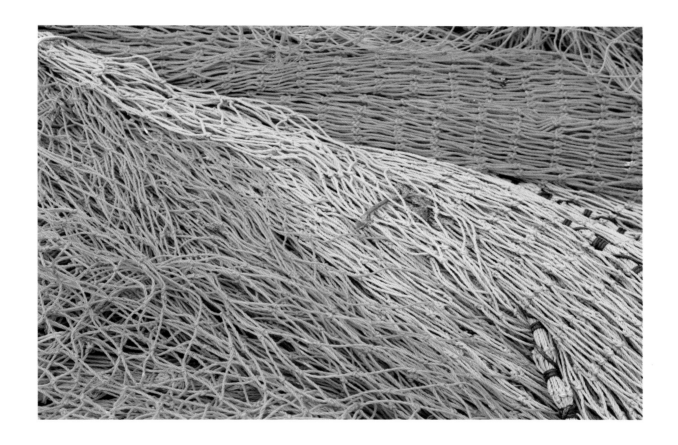

Graphic shapes in these orange fishing nets.

A colourful tangle of ropes and net washed up on the shore.

Looking across Dunmanus Bay from Ahakista at daybreak.

A vivid sunset at Reenmore, Dunmanus Bay.

A swirl of fishing nets.

A calm evening over Dunmanus from near Kilcrohane.

What looked at first like small pebbles on the seashore, turned out to be a mass of Periwinkle shells.

Blue clouds hang over Beara as I photograph
the small lighthouse Sheep's Head.

Autumn light at Glenroon, way out on the Sheep's Head peninsula on the southern side of Bantry Bay.

Amazing West Cork weather. Bright sunlight shines on the shoreline near Gortnakilly pier, whilst wild clouds burst over the Beara peninsula.

After a dark and brooding day, the sun finally makes
an appearance for last light over Bantry Bay.

Quartz.

Looking over to Whiddy island on a blue sky Autumn day from the wonderfully named Iskanafeelna, off the Glengarriff road.

Above and opposite - Two extraordinary sunsets over Glengarriff Harbour, taken from very similar positions but on different evenings. I had to include them both.

At Ellen's Rock on the Castletownbere road outside Glengarriff.

Looking through the trees at the shingle beach at Seal Harbour.

A perfect rock pool.

A stormy evening near Adrigole with Hungry Hill enveloped by cloud.

Lobster pots.

An abstract view of an amazing sky near Black Ball Head as the sun sets on an evening in winter.

The small jetty at Cahermore is almost covered by the
high tide as the light fades on a late Autumn night.

127

Like a bar of gold this lichen encrusted rock points out towards Dursey Island on a bright morning.

Another view of Dursey from across Dursey Sound on a cold and wild dawn.

The rock strewn Garnish beach on a beautiful day.

Waves sweep around a rock in Garnish Bay.

Looking across at Allihies with the Slieve Miskish mountains in the background.

When I woke up it was still dark and the rain lashed the window. I took a chance and went down to Ballydonegan beach below Allihies. As the sun started to come up the rain stopped and the remaining hazy mist grew pink with the first signs of light.

A wonderful rainbow seen from the road out of Allihies.

Waves push in and the sky catches the light from the rising sun at a small cove on the road out to Cod's Head.

After heavy rain a stream pushes through the peaty ground and drops to the sea forty feet below.

A blue dawn near Cod's Head.

A view of Reenmore Point from the road to Eyeries, just after the sun has cleared the mountains.

The small pier at Travaud at sunrise.

Rusted chains.

A cloudless dawn near Urhan.

Kelp and pebbles.

A spectacular sunset at the strand below Eyeries.

A small but perfect wave curls as it reaches the shore.

Relics from the past on the Ring of Beara.

Boats at the small pier in Argroom Harbour are dwarfed by the mountains.

A vivid orange sunset near Ardgroom.

PATRONS

Many thanks to all who decided to become
Patrons of this book. I hope you enjoy my
view of this special place.

Gordon Adair

Bob & Siobhan Allen

Patrick & Fionnuala Allen

Mohd & Ayesha Anwer

Bandon Books, Bandon, Co. Cork

Claire Barrett

David Barry

James Barry

Kathleen Barry

Keith & Antoinette Barry

Norma Bartlett

Ross & Eithne Bartley

Eleanor Bateman

Stan & Denise Beamish

Anita Begley

Victor & Suzan Bennett

Colin Blackwell

James Blackwell-Landis

Stephen Bloor

Nicolas Borkmann

Violet Boyd

William Boyd Hull

Billie Mary Brennan

Ian & Sue Burchett

Helen Burke Photography Agency Services

Clodagh Byron

Denis & Mary Cahalane

Mick Campbell

Vincent Campbell

Leslie Carr

Dominic & Helen Cashman

John Cassidy

Colum & Linda Christal

Don & Catriona Coakley

Claire Collins

Máirtina Collins

Trevor Collins

Miranda Cook

Mark & Mairead Coombes

Mary Cooney

Patrick & Linda Cosgrave

Peter Cox Photography

John Creedon

Owen Crotty, Orthodontist,

Douglas Rd., Cork

Owen & Kerry Crotty

Anna-Maria Crowley Reynolds

John Cullen

Lynn Daley, I.N.F.F, Manch,

Ballineen, Co. Cork

Robert Daley

Sylvia Daley

Carmel Daly

Lillie Daly

Mervyn Daly

Phil Davis

JoAnne Deane

Stephen De Foubert

Gef & Avril Dickson

Charlie & Catriona Dinneen

Kate & Dominic Dodd

Ciaran Dolan

Joe & Paula Dolan

Marie Downing

Ann Dunne

Eddie Dunne

Niall & Michelle Dunne

East Cork Camera Club

Deirdre Edmunds

Damian Edwardes

Mrs. H. Elwood

Michael & Moira Feen

Michael Fenton

Michael Finn

Barry Flynn

Thrésè Flynn

Foley's Pub, Castle St., Sligo

Michael & Eileen Foley

Triona Foley

Eddie Foyle

Mark & Trish Gannon

Richie Gavin

Cepa Giblin

Karen Godsil

Eddie & Ann Goggin

Hilary Good

Ralph Gordon

Les Hanlon

Kevin & Beth Hanly

Donal Harrington, Harrington's Pharmacy, Timoleague, Bandon, Co. Cork

Alan & Anna Harrison

David & Sukhi Harrison

Douglas Harrison

Richard Harrison

Hart's Coffee Shop, Clonakilty, Co. Cork

Stacy & Doug Hattori

Nuala Haydon

Garrett Hayes

Fr. Tom Hayes

Dinny & Scotty Healy

Mack & Suzan Hicks

Irene Higgins

Jacqueline Higgins

Mr. P.D. Hirons

Randal Howlett

Donald & Jane Hull

Norma Hurley

Nigel Jenkinson

Sean Jennings

Kathleen Jones

Una, Conor, Cian & Eimear Kavanagh

Gerardine Kelly

Vincent Kelly

Dallan & Tamsyn Kenny

Rose Kenny

Paddy Keogh

Fiona & DJ Keohane

Debbie & Liam King

Ian & Alma King

Harold & Voilet Kingston

Morgan & Irene Kingston

Carsten Krieger

La Modeliste, Bandon, Co. Cork

Andy & Julie Lamb

Donald Lamb

Pat & David Lamb

Clive Landis

Henry Landis

Lynn & Nicolas Lascar

Geoffrey & Judy Lean

Ivan Lee

Maureen Lee

Dr. J. A. Leigh

Ivan Leopold

Ruth & John Levis

Mary & George Lordan

Mike Louw Photography

Helen & Rex Lovell

Michael & Helen Lyne

David Lyons

Conor MacGillycuddy

Nicholas & Rosemary MacGillycuddy

Rory & Amanda MacGillycuddy

Madison, Clonakilty, Co. Cork

George Maguire

Mark & Marianne Mahaffey

Dr. Mehreen Mahmud

Tom Maloney

Marie & Brian Manning

Marketshare Enterprizes Ltd.

Catherine C. McCarthy

Donal & Nora McCarthy

Fergal & Theresa McCarthy

Dr. Katy McCarthy

Mark McCarthy

Una & Declan McCarthy

Winnie & Kevin McCarthy

Paddy & Rita McCormack

Frank McGloin

Sonia McLeish & Rolf Reimer

Fr. James Mc Sweeney

Siobhán Mc Sweeney

Sean Meehan

Juliet & Patrick Molitor

Harold & Joan Molloy

John & Lillian Morton

Jim & Deirdre Mountjoy

Kevin Murphy

Phil Murphy

John Murray, Crossing The Line Films

John & Michelle Neville

Adrian Newcombe

Susie Nicholson

Ursula Ní Luasaigh

Eileen & Tony Nolan

Patrick Noonan

Michael & Marian O'Brien

Brendan & Majella O'Callaghan

Janette O'Callaghan

David O'Carroll

Gerry O'Carroll

Gearóid agus Blánaid Ó Catháin

Michael O'Connor

Rory & Trish O'Connor

Diarmuid & Julie Ó Dálaigh

Declan O'Doherty

Mark O'Hagan

Fachtna Ó hAnnracháin

Donal & Hélène O'Hare

Jim O'Keeffe, T.D.

Eithne O'Mahony

Kevin & Maureen O'Mahony

Maureen & Dan O'Mahony

Patrick O'Meara Photography, Co. Meath

Elaine O'Neill

Ursula O'Neill

Mark O'Rourke

Deirdre & John O'Sullivan

Mike O'Sullivan & Fiona Brennan

Mrs. Rosemary O'Sullivan

Yvonne O'Sullivan

Nick Paris

Graham & Linda Perrott

Ysabel Pheifer

Photography Ireland, Mark Tracey

Jeremy Piet

Mary Pyne

Brian Reeves

Julie Rose

Sally Rowe

John Ryan

Liam Ryan

Clive Salter

Richard & Karen Salter-Townshend

Robert & Freda Salter-Townshend

Barry & June Scannell

Irene Schooling

Diana Scott

Sean & Nell

Henry Sheridan

Shirley Shorten

Yvonne Shorten

Eva Spillane

Gloria Stafford

Phyllis Stafford

Strand Framing, Clonakilty, Co. Cork

Brendan & Andrea Sullivan

David & Eithne Sullivan

Sully

Thomas Tattan

The Celtic Ross Hotel

The Opinion, Bandon, Co. Cork

The Pink Elephant, Kilbrittain, Co. Cork

Bruce & Bláithín Thompson

Maureen Thompson

Thu

Robert & Laura Travers

Maria Van Loon

Annette & Aidan Walsh

David Walsh

Ellen Walsh

Pat Walsh, Walsh's Carpets, Townspark, Midleton, Co. Cork

Donal & Jenny Warren

Jordan & Holly Warren

Sue Watterson

Marcus & Jinnie Webb

Ms. J. White

Janis White

John & Julianne Williamson

Rose Wolf

Wycherley Family

Photography Notes

For those who might be interested, I always write a little piece in my books about the way I work, the equipment I use and the thoughts I have about the process of making photographs. These are only my thoughts and photography has become so popular recently that there are an almost infinite number of opinions and methods of working, both in camera and in digital post production. I don't think I will ever reach the point where I consider myself an expert as I am also learning constantly. Consequently these are only my opinions and you can take them or leave them at will. The true test is whether or not you enjoy my images.

On photography in general.

We are now firmly in the era of digital photography and the cameras and technology we use have progressed in leaps and bounds over the last ten years or so. Hardly a month goes by without one of the main manufacturers announcing a new world beating digital camera. During this period of development, it seems that photography in general has also gone through a massive change. The number of people who now count photography as a main hobby or pastime has increased exponentially it seems. My feeling is that this has happened primarily because of this transition to digital. The idea that we can now see our pictures within seconds of making them has without doubt made it more accessible to everybody and many more people seem to be making images on a regular basis. The financial boom years of the mid 2000's also meant that people seemed to have more disposable income. Couple this with the increase in quality and the

decrease in prices of serious cameras and more people than ever purchased a "proper" SLR camera. World travel became cheap and everybody wanted to bring home top quality memories from their fantastic trip.

Is this all good? For the most part I think so. With a high volume of people buying digital cameras, the manufacturers should be continually encouraged to produce better cameras on a regular basis and invest more money in improving the technology. This is good for all photographers. The cost benefit is now much greater too. In the early days digital cameras were expensive and only those who shot thousands of images each year would reap the benefit of going digital. Nowadays the cameras are more affordable and the cost of film and processing is now easily recouped by shooting on a digital chip. Many photographers now take full control of their images from the moment of capture to when the final print is made. We no longer need to rely on others to make prints of our great visions. No need to spend time finding an expert printer and give them detailed instructions on where to dodge and burn, what level of contrast to use and what our preferred paper is. No need to find an extra room in which to set up our own smelly darkroom, just a space for a small table on which to place our digital darkroom with printer included. No need to get our hands wet! Add this to our new found ability to assess images at the exact moment we make them, there is without doubt no good reason to use film for most people. Finally, we can now share our pictures with the entire world just minutes after making them. A few clicks of the mouse and they are uploaded to our own web sites, the social networks or both. Relatives in other parts of the world can share our memories with ease. Without doubt this is fantastic progress and all in just a few short years.

So is there a downside? It's hard to know and I don't want to be a critic. However, I feel that perhaps there are two things happening that may be bad for photography. The first is that we are perhaps becoming over saturated with photographic images. Many would argue that history can be told more effectively with images and that the more images we have, the more that history is recorded for future generations. I would not dispute this. It is also easy to convey ideas, display places or products and share memories with photographic images. The concern I have is that everyone now believes that most digital images have been manipulated after they are taken and there is often almost no trust in the reality of images anymore. This is probably more true in the realms of celebrity photography whether it is an airbrushed portrait or a paparazzi style image where people are seen doing things they shouldn't! In many cases there may be foundation to this distrust but it is a pity that if you spend time in the environment making an image of a spectacular sunset that it will be assumed that it has been "photo shopped". This brings me to the second small problem. We photographers may indeed be guilty of "over working" our images. There is no doubt that there are many images now which seem unreal and I feel we must be careful in how we represent the world, particularly in the spectrum of environmental photography. With early digital cameras the results were often disappointing and so had to be enhanced to become good representations of what the true scene looked like. Newer models often give almost too much saturation to images and therefore they can look manipulated from the start. The tools we now have at our disposal in terms of digital software make almost anything possible but without doubt the best images are the ones made when conditions are right and little or no work needs to be done. Because of the way digital images are captured it is almost always necessary to do some post processing but it is easy to get sucked into over doing them. If a sky is not interesting enough we can simply "drop one in" from a previous photo. For illustration purposes this may be fine but for me the greatest pleasure comes from being there when our planet does its own wonderful thing.

Equipment and working methods.

My first book "Ireland's Wildlife - A Photographic Essay" 2002, was shot entirely on film. Digital SLR cameras were around by that time but they were still in the very early stages of development even when I was finishing the project. They were great for news work where pictures needed to be moved across the world quickly, with quality being a secondary consideration. However, they were not really up to the standard of film for more detailed work. Things were moving fast though and by the time I published my second book "Images of Irish Nature" 2006, I had "gone digi" and apart from one or two images that I used from my library of film images, they were all made on one of two digital cameras that I was using by then.

The images in this book were for the most part made on digital cameras. However, there are a few which are from my pre-digital days. In those days I was concentrating more on pure wildlife images but I always had an eye on the landscape and made images of it when I got the opportunity. The film images were made with a Bronica ETRS 6x4.5 cm camera. As a wildlife photographer I had large collection of 35 mm equipment with me all the time but as I also had the Bronica for other assignments, I tended to use this larger format for the landscapes I shot. I sometimes regret not moving up to the wonderful 5"x4" format as an image shot on transparency in that format is just so beautiful. With the Bronica I used just two prime lenses, the 75 mm standard and a 40 mm wide angle. For most of my work these were ample and to be honest, when using digital cameras I rarely use focal lengths that are different from these. With the speed that digital technology has moved it is inevitable that we all want to change cameras regularly to keep up

with improvements in image quality and I have been no different. In total I have used four different digital cameras for the images for this project, along with the Bronica. I started my digital career with the Canon 1Ds which to be honest was probably too early in the game. While it had a reasonable pixel count of just over 11 megapixels the quality of the images was not fantastic. Noise in the darker areas could be a problem and also in images which required extended shutter speeds. However, there are a good number of images in this book which were made on that camera and I feel they stand up to scrutiny very well. The Canon 1D Mk2 was my next digital purchase and this was primarily used for my wildlife work. It was a speed machine in comparison to the 1Ds and so was more suited to my nature work but I did use it for one of the landscape images in this book. It is a camera with just 8.2 megapixels but for the image in question I just felt it would be more suitable than the 1Ds. The quality of the particular image is so good that I regularly do 24"x16" prints from it. Which image is it? Have a look through the book and see if you can guess!

The Canon 5D replaced my 1Ds and it is a camera that I have been extremely happy with. I chose it over the 1Ds Mk2 as I was looking for a camera to do my wedding work with as well as my illustrative work. As such it was a lighter camera to carry around for long periods and although it had less megapixels than the 1Ds Mk2, the image quality was excellent. I still use the 5D for landscape work at times as I find it pleasing to work with and it has a wonderfully forgiving file with great dynamic range. My latest acquisition was the 1Ds Mk3. With 21 megapixels it truly is a phenomenal performer. However there are times when I find the 5D suits a particular situation better. The Mk3 has gone the way of most of the more recent cameras in that the colour saturation in the files is now much higher than it used to be. This can be great for low light situations where colours are more muted but on high contrast days with full-on colour, I find it can overdo things a little. This is personal taste and others may love the strength of the images but often I find them a little aggressive. However, on a evening with pastel skies and soft tones, or for situations where maximum detail is required it is an excellent choice.

The three lenses I use for landscape work are all zooms which a few years ago would be unheard of. Prime lenses would have been the only choice for shots requiring detail to be shown but nowadays the quality of the better zoom lenses is up to most jobs. The lenses I use are the 17 to 40 mm F4, the 24 to 70 mm F2.8 and the 70 to 200 mm F2.8 Canon L series lenses. The one I use most often is definitely the 24 to 70 mm F2.8, again personal choice. On full frame digital cameras I like the range of this lens and its the one I would keep if ever I was limited to just one lens. Occasionally I pull out the 17 to 40 mm if I am either confined to a tight space or I need a wider option to exaggerate perspective a little. I use the 70-200 mm F2.8 for shooting the longer views to isolate detail. I like the standard 35 mm format of the digital cameras but don't let them inhibit me from creating images of different shapes through cropping. The panoramic shots in this book are mainly cropped from the original format although one image is the result of stitching two images together to produce the same result. It is slow work and if possible I will shoot one image and crop.

There is not one single image in this book which was shot without the use of a tripod. When teaching or speaking to camera clubs this is my most consistent piece of advice. Always use a tripod. It will be slower, which can make getting a grab shot of a sudden sunset more difficult but the benefit in sharpness will always show. Slowing down also helps you concentrate on how you are composing a shot and hopefully yields a better final result. On top of a sturdy tripod I use a geared head. They are wonderful for getting precise compositions and help immensely with rigidity too. They are also a little slower to use than conventional three way heads or ball and socket heads but in my opinion are far superior to either. A double bubble spirit level that fits into the hot shoe of the camera keeps the horizon straight and a cable release for releasing the shutter is always on hand. The final piece of important equipment for my landscape work is a set of graduated filters. I use Lee grads in both hard and soft gradations and from one to three stops in each. They are essential to me for balancing the light between foreground and sky in some exposures. Much easier to do this in camera than messing around in photoshop afterwards. They require practice to use and again they can slow you down but they are an effective tool.

Most of my work is planned. I often go to locations many times before I actually make an image. Seeing a coastal location with different light and at different times of year and in different weather gives you the information you need to know when it should be best for photography. The tides will of course be of great importance too on coastal locations. I make notes if necessary and when the weather is right and I can get out, I can assess which location offers the most possibilities. Early morning and the last few hours of the day are always going to be the best. The world just looks right then. Dragging myself out of bed is often the hardest part, particularly in the summer months when sunrise is really early. It does make the difference though as once the sun gets up too high you can put the camera away until late in the evening. During the shorter months of the year it is sometimes possible to work through the day more easily as the sun stays relatively low in the sky but early and late in the day is still usually best. If I get one good image from a landscape session I am happy. It is slow work and you must be patient. Sometimes the weather changes unexpectedly. At times this helps and at times it doesn't but if you are not there you can't make a picture. Many times I have watched an afternoon progress and expected great things, only to be disappointed as clouds bubble up on the western horizon to block off the evening sun just when the light should be getting to its best.

Since my interest in landscape photography began I have been happy to follow the advice of the great landscape photographers of our time. Joe Cornish, David Noton and many others advise on using simple yet effective procedures to get the most from your images. When I read these tips first they were based towards large format or panoramic cameras but they are as relevant now with digital photography as they ever were. Camera on tripod, spirit level in place, cable release attached, filter in position if necessary, mirror lock up engaged and wait for the light. When it looks good, meter and shoot. With film it was advised that you bracket your exposures to be sure of the perfect image. With digital we can now check our exposure after the first image and make any small adjustments

necessary for the next and subsequent shots. In some situations there may be many chances of a great image. The light looks good and then it just gets better and better before finally dying away. At other times you may have to work quickly and make one hasty exposure before the best light is gone - such is landscape photography.

And finally the processing. Photoshop is the program I use for my processing with Adobe Camera Raw for converting the Raw images. Subtle changes during the raw processing stage can leave very little work needed in Photoshop. I find that the best images generally need the least attention anyway. Digital cameras do have shortcomings however and I will use some simple methods to extend the dynamic range of an image at times. I don't use full-on HDR techniques on images though, as I find they always look unreal. If there is strong light in one area of an image there will inevitably be strong shadow in another. It is our job as photographers to find the best way of recording this. I have seen so many ways of doing things to images and each person who uses them swears they are both the best and the least destructive, its hard to know what is correct at times. I use different methods on different occasions from a variety of sources. My only criteria is that the final image should look as close to how I remember the scene as possible. If I can accomplish that I am happy.

Enjoy your photography.

ACKNOWLEDGEMENTS

To all those who have helped with the organising of this project or with my business in general I offer my heartfelt thanks. To others who have simply encouraged me over the years with words of support or their love of my work, I also wish to express my deepest gratitude. Without you all I would never get to make any of my images. This book is for you.

A special thanks go to the following people.
To my mum Annabel for all her fantastic support and belief over the years. To my sister Kate and Pat, to Mel and Ben, Siobhan and Gordon and all my other family members for their encouragement. To Terry, Carole and Billy at the hotel in Courtmac where this all started. To my parents in law Leon and Josée who are always there for us. To Bart, Gerda, Kris and their families for their continued support. To my late grandparents Dennis and Patricia who brought me to this wonderful place but sadly won't see this book. To Ramona who designed this book so beautifully and who puts up with me changing my mind so well, and for her work in all other departments of my business. To Liz who runs my life at the Gallery for all her fantastic help, encouragement and organisation. To Patryk Lubas for his assistance and guidance with this project. To my friend Caroline for her support and for feeding me at times when on location. To Jeremy, Pete, Andy and Stevie for their friendship. To Declan and Siorcha for their consistent encouragement. To fellow photographers Eddie Dunne and Billy Clarke who are always supportive.

To the Sponsors, Commercial Patrons and individual Patrons of this book I wish to say a special thanks. Your help and trust is what makes these books possible.

Finally to my amazing wife and best friend Rita. To our family, Matthew, Rosie, Brad and Sarah and of course Vinny. I cannot express how much I love you all and how much your love means to me.